WHAT'S THE BIG IDEA?

MONEY
and
TRADE

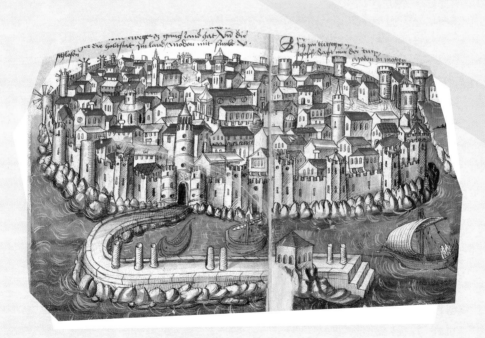

Tim Cooke

Cavendish
Square

New York

Published in 2018 by Cavendish Square Publishing, LLC
243 5th Avenue, Suite 136 New York, NY 10016

Website: cavendishsq.com

This publication represents the opinions and views of the author based on his or her personal experiences, knowledge, and research. The information in this book serves as a general guide only. The author and publisher have used their best efforts in preparing this book and disclaim liabilty rising directly or indirectly for the use and application of this book.

CPSIA compliance information: Batch #CS17CSQ.

All websites were available and accurate when this book went to press.

Library of Congress Cataloging-in-Publication Data

Names: Cooke, Tim.
Title: Money and trade / Tim Cooke.
Description: New York : Cavendish Square, 2018. | Series: What's the big idea? | Includes index.
Identifiers: ISBN 9781502628169 (library bound) | ISBN 9781502628176 (ebook)
Subjects: LCSH: Commerce--Juvenile literature. | Free trade--Juvenile literature. | International trade--Juvenile literature. | Money--Juvenile literature.
Classification: LCC HF353.C66 2018 | DDC 382--dc23

For Brown Bear Books Ltd:
Managing Editor: Tim Cooke
Editorial Director: Lindsey Lowe
Designer: Supriya Sahai
Design Manager: Keith Davis
Children's Publisher: Anne O'Daly
Picture Manager: Sophie Mortimer

Picture Credits:
Front Cover: Janis Christie/Digital Vision/Getty Images
Interior: 123rf: 12-13, Andrey Armyagov 41, Sergey Tsvetkov 20; **Dreamstime:** 8, DVMS Images 15; **Getty Images:** Corbis 36-37; **Library of Congress:** 26, 27, 29, 33; **NARA:** 38; **Public Domain:** 16, 21, Gavin Collins 14, Louvre Museum 4, PHGCOM/Tokyo Currency Museum 17; **Shutterstock:** 10, 11, Everett Historical 23, 28, 35, 39, Glynnis Jones 40; **Thinkstock:** istockphoto 5, 6-7, 22, Photos.com 24-25, 30-31, 32, 34.

All other photos artwork and maps, Brown Bear Books.

Brown Bear Books has made every attempt to contact the copyright holder.
If you have any information please contact licensing@brownbearbooks.co.uk

Manufactured in the United States of America

CONTENTS

INTRODUCTION

Trade has shaped international relations for many thousands of years. It stimulated exploration, the spread of ideas, and the creation of empires.

Trade is virtually as old as humankind. The earliest peoples swapped meat or fur with their neighbors in return for other things they needed, such as fish or cooking vessels. As people began to settle in villages, markets grew. The invention of money encouraged the growth of trade. Money overcame the inconvenience of having to **barter** for goods. By the time of the Greek and Roman empires from the 400s BCE, trade routes joined Europe to Asia.

This illustration shows a visit by officials of the Republic of Venice to Syria in the 1500s. The Venetians wanted to encourage trade with the Muslim state of Syria.

London is one of the world's most important financial centers. Other important cities include New York City, Singapore, Hong Kong, and Tokyo.

After the rise of Islam in the Middle East, Europeans tried to find new trade routes to East Asia. In the 1500s and 1600s, this exploration led to the creation of European **colonies** in the Americas, Asia, and Africa.

Growth of free trade

The first study of economic theory was *The Wealth of Nations*, published by Adam Smith in 1776. Smith said governments should leave trade to regulate, or manage, itself. Trade should be controlled by the laws of **supply and demand**, rather than by governments. Smith's theory has dominated **economics** ever since, with various adjustments. Some economists have suggested alternatives to a **free market**, such as **communism**, in which a government controls all economic activity. However, free-market economics continue to dominate the global economy in the 2010s.

THE ORIGINS OF TRADE

Ever since prehistoric people learned how to hunt and gather food, people have swapped things they have for things they need.

These exchanges were the start of trade. People were making informal trade deals about 20,000 years ago, and probably even before that. At the time, people still lived a **nomadic** lifestyle. They may have swapped beautiful feathers for animal skins, or meat for flint tools. By 12,000 BCE, trade had become more organized. In the Mediterranean, experts have discovered ancient trade routes by studying finds of a rock

RIVER TRADE

Boats called feluccas have been used to carry goods on the Nile River for thousands of years.

called obsidian. Obsidian is a hard, black volcanic rock that can be sharpened to make knives or tools. It only occurs naturally in a few places, but experts have found obsidian objects all around the Mediterranean. They must have been distributed along ancient trade routes.

Early traders

Beginning in Mesopotamia (modern-day Iraq) in about 8000 BCE, people learned to grow crops and began to settle in villages. Over centuries, farmers began to grow more crops than they needed. Villagers began to swap their produce or things they had made. Markets began where people met to exchange goods. People might swap goat meat for a clay pot, or a piece of woven cloth for a loaf of bread. Money did not yet exist, so goods were exchanged for other goods or services, a process known as barter. Some people became merchants. They began to travel long distances to bring unusual and valuable goods back to sell in the markets.

TIMELINE

ca. 12,000 BCE Obsidian is traded widely from its sources in Anatolia (modern Turkey) and a few Mediterranean islands.

ca. 3000 BCE Trade is well established on many of the rivers of the ancient world, including the Nile in Egypt, the Indus in India, and the Yellow River in China.

ca. 1000 BCE Traders establish overland routes across Asia, including the Silk Road, which connects China and South Asia to the Mediterranean Sea.

The earliest known organized traders were the Sumerians of Mesopotamia. About 5,000 years ago, they traded with the Harappan people of the Indus Valley in what is now Pakistan. Sumerian merchants traveled long distances to buy and sell goods. They sometimes used barley as a form of payment.

The first trade routes

Between 3000 and 1000 BCE, trade was carried out along the great rivers of the world such as the Nile in Egypt, the Tigris and Euphrates in Mesopotamia, the Indus in India, and the Yellow River in China. It was quicker and easier to transport goods by boat than on land. At the time, most cultures still did not have any wheeled transport. The ancient Phoenicians of present-day Lebanon in the eastern Mediterranean were great sea traders. Their cedar wood was highly prized for boat building because it was light and watertight.

CEDAR WOOD

Cedar wood forests gave the Phoenicians something valuable to trade.

Early trade vessels had sails, but they also carried rowers in case the wind was blowing in the wrong direction.

The Phoenicians also produced another highly prized purple dye that came from sea snails. The dye was so valuable in ancient Rome that only the emperor wore clothes dyed with it. Wearing purple was a sign of his wealth and power.

In around 110 BCE, ancient Greek sailors discovered trade winds. These winds blew steadily in set directions near the equator. Sailors could rely on them to make voyages to the east or west.

EARLY TRADE NETWORKS

Experts have traced early trade networks. Some of these networks carried goods over long distances.

1. Baltic tribes sold amber to Romans

2. Romans sold weapons to Baltic tribes

3. Greeks sold pottery and wine to Etruscans

4. India sold spices and silks (from China) to Romans

5. Hittites sold iron to Egyptians

With the discovery of trade winds, sailors began to make voyages across open water instead of hugging the coastline. They also had better ships. The Greeks were skilled at **metallurgy**. By using nails rather than plant fibers to fasten the wooden timbers of their ships, they built vessels that could withstand storms at sea.

Land routes

From around 1000 BCE, traders in Asia and Africa began to carry goods on land routes. They could do this thanks to the camel. People discovered that the camel was ideally suited to living in the desert. It could go for long periods without water and needed little food. They could also carry heavy goods over long distances. The invention of a saddle to place over the camel's hump meant traders could ride instead of walking with their goods. For safety from attack by thieves or wild animals, traders traveled long distances in large groups known as caravans.

CARAVAN

Camels cross the desert in large groups called caravans. They can survive for up to six months without food. They live on fat stored in their humps.

←

RUINS

Jiaohe was once a stopping-off point for merchants on the Silk Road in the hot, dry desert near China's western border.

The Silk Road

One of the oldest and most important trade routes was the Silk Road, which connected China and India to Europe through Central Asia. The Silk Road was actually a number of overland routes that eventually stretched a total of 4,000 miles (6,400 km) across deserts and mountain ranges. The Han Dynasty (207 BCE–220 CE) used it to send silk merchants over land toward Europe. In the west, the Silk Road ended at the Mediterranean Sea in modern Turkey. From there, goods such as silk and spices were carried on ships to Rome and other European ports.

IN SUMMARY

■ Trade took place over long routes before people began to live in settled communities.

■ The growth of agriculture led to the development of markets for the exchange of **surplus** produce.

■ Early goods were mainly transported by water.

THE INVENTION OF MONEY

As early people began to travel over longer distances, it became more difficult to rely on barter for trade.

Barter depends on both traders wanting what the other person has. To try to make sure this was the case, traders carried **commodities** that were in high demand. The Sumerians used barley as payment. Salt was also used to pay for goods. Salt was rare, but early peoples needed it to preserve and flavor food.

COINAGE

The first coins appeared in the 600s BCE. They were stamped with rulers' heads and other symbols as a sign that they were genuine. →

Other goods used for payment before money existed included shells, feathers, and animal teeth, which were all used to make jewelry. Native Americans often traded tobacco leaves and blankets.

Trading with silver

Relying on different sorts of payment was difficult. Salt melted if it got wet, and blankets were heavy to carry. Sumerian merchants knew that barley might go rotten during a long journey. Instead, they started to trade using something that could not go bad. The Sumerians had access to deposits of silver. In other places, however, silver was rare, which made it valuable. From about 3000 BCE, the Sumerians melted silver into **ingots** for trade. This was one of the first forms of money. To make sure silver was accurately weighed, the Sumerians used official units of weight called shekels. The word shekel is still sometimes used as an informal term for money.

TIMELINE

ca. 3000 BCE
The Sumerians begin to use silver ingots for trade. Silver is weighed in official units called shekels.

ca. 640 BCE
The Lydians in what is now Turkey make the world's first coins. The coins carry a stamped lion, the symbol of the Lydian king, as a sign that they are genuine.

600s CE
The Chinese begin printing the first paper money. It is initially created by mechants as receipts, but is later printed by the government.

As the Sumerians traveled and came into contact with different people, the idea of using silver as payment for goods spread. Merchants from other cultures began to use silver for trade.

Invention of coins

The first coins appeared in Lydia (modern-day Turkey) in 640 BCE. They were made of electrum, a mixture of gold and silver. The coins were bean shaped and each was stamped with a lion's head. The lion was the symbol of the king of Lydia, so people trusted that they contained an exact weight of pure gold and silver. Within 100 years, ancient Greeks and Persians were also using coins for trade. Later, the Romans introduced standardized coins across their growing empire.

Coins are a great help to modern archaeologists because they are stamped with evidence of where they were made. The lion was used in Lydia, in Athens the symbol was an owl, and the Greek islands of Andros, Ceos, and Aegina used a vase, a squid, and a turtle.

CUNEIFORM

The Sumerians invented the first form of writing to keep track of trade deals. It was called cuneiform, or "wedge shaped" because a wedge-shaped reed was used to make marks in a tablet of soft clay. →

Each Roman emperor had his picture and name on the coins he issued. Experts study the distribution of the coins of a particular emperor. They show what places were probably linked by trade routes during his reign.

Paper Money

In 1295 CE, the Venetian merchant Marco Polo returned home from years traveling in Asia. He reported seeing paper money in China. People in Europe did not yet use paper money. They only trusted gold and silver coins.

THE COMING OF PAPER MONEY

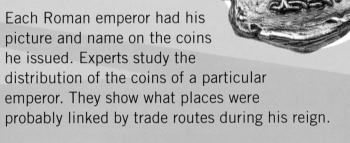

Paper money was invented in China in the early Middle Ages. It was another century before paper banknotes were used in the West.

China **600s**
Sweden **1661**
England **1694**
Norway **1695**
France **1718**
Scotland **1723**

Unlike other countries, China did not have a ready supply of gold and silver or, later, copper to turn into coins. Instead, the Chinese made coins from iron. But iron was so heavy that people were reluctant to carry money. Instead, Chinese merchants issued handwritten **receipts** to say that people had left a certain number of coins with them. Eventually, people began to use those receipts to buy goods. Anyone given the receipt could collect the coins from the merchant if they wanted to. Early in the 1000s, the Chinese government took over for the merchants. The government started to print official receipts that could be used as money.

These first banknotes brought together a number of Chinese inventions. The Chinese had invented paper 1,000 years before Marco Polo had visited the country. They had also invented a method of printing with woodblocks a few hundred years later. The Chinese also found it easy to accept the idea that a banknote had value, even though it was not made of a valuable material.

MERCHANT

The Venetian merchant Marco Polo reported seeing paper money in China long before it was introduced in Europe. →

16

BANKNOTES

The Chinese printed the first official paper money in the 600s. The designs were complex to prevent people printing their own banknotes.

←

Chinese merchants were used to doing business on **credit**. Goods were bought or sold on the understanding that payments would be made in the future. Buyers and sellers did not exchange coins, but instead issued paper receipts.

Back to the past

Today, it is possible to buy almost anything without using paper money or coins. Even plastic credit cards are unnecessary. People buy things using a smartphone or a virtual **currency** that does not exist. **Bitcoin** is used on the Internet for buying and selling.

IN SUMMARY

- Money emerged from the need to overcome various disadvantages of the barter system.

- Coins originally contained precious metals, so they had an actual value. Because paper has no value, the value of banknotes was symbolic.

EUROPEAN TRADE ROUTES

After the wealth and success of the Roman Empire, European trade declined for hundreds of years during the Dark Ages.

Trade was at the heart of the success of the Roman Empire. The Romans controlled sea routes in the Mediterranean and Black Seas. They built roads across their empire so that goods could be easily transported. A single currency was used across the empire, and there were no taxes on trade. Rome traded with its provinces in Spain, France, England, the Middle East, and North Africa.

VIKINGS

The Vikings of Scandinavia developed special cargo ships called cogs that they used on the rivers and seas of northern Europe.

All kinds of goods were imported to Rome itself. Beef, corn, metals, leather, glassware, marble, olive oil, purple dye, spices, timber, and wine arrived at Rome's port, Ostia, about 15 miles (24 km) from Rome on the Tiber River.

Dark Ages

In 476, the Roman emperor in the West was overthrown by a Germanic people. The Roman Empire collapsed—and so did its trade routes. Sea travel became dangerous for traders. Without Roman warships to keep order, pirates operated in the Mediterranean and along the Atlantic coast.

Europe's economy slowed down. For centuries, trade was mainly local. But from the 700s, Vikings from Scandinavia established a new trade network using the rivers of northern Europe. They took slaves, fur, and amber from Russia to the Black Sea, where they sold goods to the Byzantines in Constantinople (present-day Istanbul) and to the Islamic caliphate in Baghdad.

TIMELINE

700s Viking traders open trade routes around the coasts of northern Europe and via rivers into what is now Russia.

1000s The Republic of Venice controls the Adriatic Sea, allowing it to build an empire based on trade with Islamic states in the eastern Mediterranean.

1492 Trying to find a new sea route to Asia, Christopher Columbus sails to the Caribbean, opening trade routes between Europe and the Americas.

Viking trade slowed and ended in the 1000s, but the trade networks survived. Many former Viking ports in Scandinavia and Germany came together to form the Hanseatic League. This was a formal **commercial** assocation that controlled trade in the North Sea and the Baltic.

Islamic trade routes

In the 600s, a new faith named Islam began in the Middle East. As Islam spread, Muslim trade routes stretched from the Arabian Peninsula to southern Spain and North Africa. Other important routes led south to West Africa. Traders carried luxury goods such as incense, silk, and spices, as well as ordinary goods such as pottery. Initially, cowrie shells were used as currency, but traders soon began to use coins and paper money.

HANSEATIC LEAGUE

German traders of the Hanseatic League built ports around the Baltic and North Seas, such as Bergen in Norway. The harbors and piers are still lined with distinctive Hansa-style warehouses. ↓

As southern Europe emerged from the Dark Ages, city-states in Italy started to trade directly with the Islamic Middle East. During the Crusades from the 1000s to the 1200s, Christian and Islamic armies fought each other for control of the Holy Land.

TRADING BASE

Methoni in Greece was a Venetian center for trade with the Islamic world. Its fortified harbor helped protect cargo ships from pirates. →

The Italian city-states continued trading with the Islamic Empire, however. The most important of these was Venice. From a **lagoon** in northern Italy, Venice created a vast **maritime** empire that lasted from the 1000s to the 1400s.

Looking for spices

One important commodity in the late Middle Ages was spices. Spices such as cinnamon and pepper added flavor to food that was bad or boring. Some spices were used as medicine.

THE TRIANGULAR TRADE

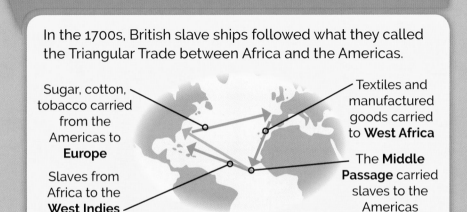

In the 1700s, British slave ships followed what they called the Triangular Trade between Africa and the Americas.

Sugar, cotton, tobacco carried from the Americas to **Europe**

Slaves from Africa to the **West Indies**

Textiles and manufactured goods carried to **West Africa**

The **Middle Passage** carried slaves to the Americas

Most spices originated in Asia, but the overland trade routes were controlled by Muslim merchants in Central Asia. As Europe enjoyed a period of relative peace in the 1400s, the rulers of Spain and Portugal sent explorers to find a new sea route to Asia. The Portuguese developed new types of sailing ships, the caravel and the carrack, that were well suited to ocean voyages.

Christopher Columbus sailed west across the Atlantic on behalf of Spain. Instead of finding a way to Asia, he discovered the Americas in 1492. This opened what became a highly valuable new trade route. Spain used slaves to work in gold and silver mines in Central and South America and became the richest country in Europe.

In 1497, the Portuguese navigator Vasco da Gama sailed round the Cape of Good Hope (the southern tip of Africa) into the Indian Ocean. His journey opened up a sea route to the so-called Spice Islands of what is now Indonesia. No longer did European traders have to pay high prices to Muslim spice traders. Thanks to their ships and guns, the Portuguese became the dominant power in the spice trade.

SPICES

Spices were one of the most valuable goods in medieval Europe. They helped to give flavor to food and were said to have medicinal benefits. →

SLAVES

African slaves were taken from Africa to North America and the Caribbean on overcrowded ships that belonged mainly to British traders.

←

A new trade

Portuguese supremacy did not last. Before long the Netherlands took over the spice trade. The Netherlands and Britain built the strongest fleets in Europe and led efforts to set up trade routes around the world. As part of the process, a new commodity emerged: African slaves. Between the mid-1500s and the late 1700s, African, Arab, and European slave traders forcibly removed more than 10 million Africans from their homes and shipped them to the Americas to work on sugar, cotton, and tobacco **plantations**.

IN SUMMARY

 Trade declined sharply in Europe after the fall of the Roman Empire.

 From the 1000s, trade grew between Europe and Asia, but Muslim control of the overland trade routes encouraged Europeans to seek new sea routes to Asia.

INDUSTRY, EMPIRE, AND TRADE

In the 1700s and 1800s, Europeans created overseas trading empires in order to find supplies and markets for their growing industries.

In 1600, a group of English **investors** formed the East India Company to trade with India. Investors in the Netherlands formed the Dutch East India Company in 1602. These private companies grew rich on Europe's demand for spices, silk, porcelain, and other goods from Asia. As the companies set up trading posts around the world, they hired soldiers to protect them.

INDUSTRY

The Industrial Revolution from the mid-1700s to the mid-1800s led to an expansion of industry and manufacture in Europe and the Americas. →

The companies grew into powerful organizations that were closely involved in the countries where they traded. The East India Company helped defend princes of the states that made up India in return for being allowed to trade. The company built roads and railroads, and acted in many ways as a form of government. It was the forerunner of large **multinational** companies of the modern age. The Dutch, meanwhile, had similar power in Indonesia and other parts of Southeast Asia.

The British Empire

Europe's governments helped to protect traders' activities, and set up their own military and naval bases. British rule later spread to South Africa, Australia, and New Zealand. The East India Company controlled nearly the whole of India by the 1850s. In 1857 its private army rebelled. The British government decided the company could no longer govern India, and took over the colony. India became the jewel of the British Empire, which at its peak in the 1920s controlled around a quarter of the world.

TIMELINE

1600
British traders form the East India Company to develop trade with India and East Asia.

1842
British victory in the First Opium War forces the Chinese to allow foreigners to trade in China. In the next decade, Japan also permits international trade.

1901
Andrew Carnegie sells the Carnegie Steel Company to J. P. Morgan for $492 million, making him at the time the richest man in America.

The rise of industry

The rise of the British Empire was helped by changes in Europe created by the Industrial Revolution. In 1800, just 3 percent of the world's population lived in a city. Most people lived in small villages, growing their own food and making their own clothes. They had little money to buy anything. A hundred years later, the urban population had grown fivefold to 15 percent. Steam engines powered machines in factories that wove cotton, molded rails for new railroads, or made steel parts for more new machines. People left the countryside to work in the new factories, and earned wages that allowed them to buy goods made in factories. They had become **consumers**.

Goods for everyone

In the past, trade had concentrated on luxury imports such as silk. Now, everyday food produce such as coffee and tea was imported. The expansion of the railroads and the invention of the refrigerated railroad car in the late 1800s transformed the beef industry.

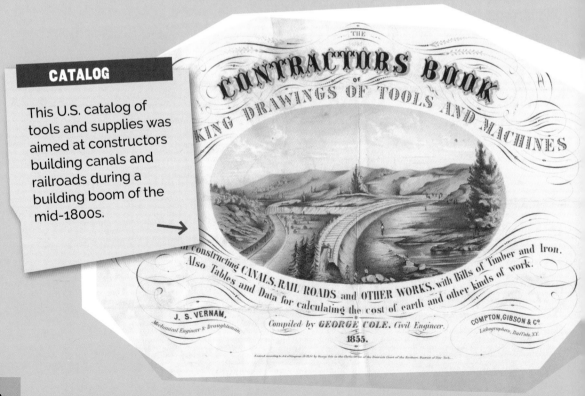

CATALOG

This U.S. catalog of tools and supplies was aimed at constructors building canals and railroads during a building boom of the mid-1800s.

STOCKYARDS

Chicago was a meat-packing center from the 1860s. Livestock brought by train from the West were killed and the meat sent on to cities on the East Coast. →

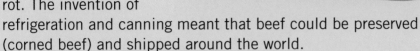

In Argentina, millions of cattle were killed for their hides and the meat was left to rot. The invention of refrigeration and canning meant that beef could be preserved (corned beef) and shipped around the world.

In the United States, a cattle industry grew up around the cowboys and **railheads** of Texas and the Great Plains. Beef was shipped by train to the growing cities of the eastern seaboard. Fresh meat became far more affordable than it had been in the past.

MAKING IT RICH

Seven of the richest Americans in history made their fortunes in business in the late 1800s. Their estimated fortunes are expressed in 2011 equivalents.

$66.1 billion	Marshall Field (retail)
$71.2 billion	Jay Gould (railroads)
$79.4 billion	Frederik Weyerhaeuser (timber)
$88.9 billion	A. T. Stewart (retail)
$185 billion	Cornelius Vanderbilt (railroads)
$309 billion	Andrew Carnegie (steel)
$336 billion	John D. Rockefeller (oil)

The power of the company

Meanwhile, European control grew in other parts of the globe. European dominance of trade allowed European countries to control trade routes and raw materials. In 1798, the Chinese emperor had dismissed a British trade delegation. Forty years later, another emperor threatened to stop the East India Company importing opium to China from India. The drug was ruining the lives of Chinese workers. British warships attacked China and forced it to give up trade concessions and territory to Britain, including Hong Kong. The British willingness to fight to protect trade had achieved positive results.

A similar incident happened in 1853. U.S. warships commanded by Commodore Matthew Perry sailed into Tokyo harbor in Japan. At the time, Japan rejected all foreign trade. Perry's appearance forced Japan to allow U.S. traders to operate at two ports. A few years later, Japan agreed to allow foreigners to trade in more locations.

OPIUM WAR

The British defeated the Chinese at the mouth of the Pearl River in 1841 during the First Opium War. The two sides clashed in a second war from 1856 to 1860.

The rise of U.S. industry

In the late 1800s, industrialization was leading to the growth of large **corporations**. This was most clearly seen in the United States. Men such as Scottish-born steel tycoon Andrew Carnegie and oil tycoon John D. Rockefeller, the richest man in America, set up businesses that became huge corporations with many interests. As the companies grew bigger, they influenced political decisions in the White House and economic decisions on Wall Street. Many critics argued that the industrialists had too much power.

MILLIONAIRE

Andrew Carnegie ➝ made a fortune from steel and railroad construction. He spent much of his later life giving his money away for charitable causes.

IN SUMMARY

■ Europeans set up colonies overseas to provide both raw materials for industry and a larger market for their products.

■ Mechanization, industry, and new transportation encouraged the growth of huge corporations.

ECONOMIC THEORIES

Ever since the beginnings of trade and the use of money, thinkers have argued whether trade is a good or bad thing.

More than 2,000 years ago, in the 300s BCE, the Greek **philosopher** Aristotle argued that earning money to support a household was a good thing, but that it was wrong to make a lot of money through trade. He was the first to argue that money had a **moral** value and not just a **functional** value.

SPANIARDS

The defeat of the Aztec by the Spanish explorer Hernán Cortés (*left*) in 1521 allowed Spain to take huge amounts of gold and silver from the Americas.

Medieval thinkers

During the Middle Ages, thinkers continued to debate questions about the morality of money and trade. In the 1200s, the Catholic scholar Saint Thomas Aquinas argued that every item had a just price, which sellers should stick to. He argued that money was a consumable product just like food, and that to make a profit from money itself went against the natural law. Aquinas's views were influential for over 300 years. The powerful Catholic Church banned Christians from charging **interest** on loans of money. It said this was a sin called usury. Jews in Europe became important moneylenders, and gained a reputation for being involved in business.

In the 1300s, the Islamic scholar Ibn Khaldun, who worked in Tunisia, had very modern ideas about money and the economy. He was one of the first people to argue that high taxes can damage an economy, for example.

TIMELINE

1500s
Envious of Spain and its gold and silver reserves from South America, European nations adopt **mercantilism** as a policy.

1776
Adam Smith publishes *The Wealth of Nations*, setting out the theory of free-market economics. The book begins the study of economics in its own right.

1848
Germans Karl Marx and Friedrich Engels publish *The Communist Manifesto*. It is widely banned and makes little initial impact.

31

Gaining wealth

From the 1500s to the 1700s, a new approach shaped trade in northern Europe. The English, French, and Dutch were jealous of the wealth of Spain, which received huge amounts of gold and silver from Mexico and South America. Governments in northern Europe also set out to amass wealth. This was called mercantilism. It reflected a belief that there was a limited amount of money in the world, and that a country's power depended on how much of the money it had. Governments set out to build reserves of gold. They discouraged people from buying imports, because that involved sending payment to other countries. Instead, **exports** that brought money into the country were encouraged.

Wealth of Nations

In 1776, the Scotsman Adam Smith published *The Wealth of Nations*. Smith's analysis of how trade worked was directly opposed to mercantilism. The book created a new economic theory and remains the most influential book ever published about economics.

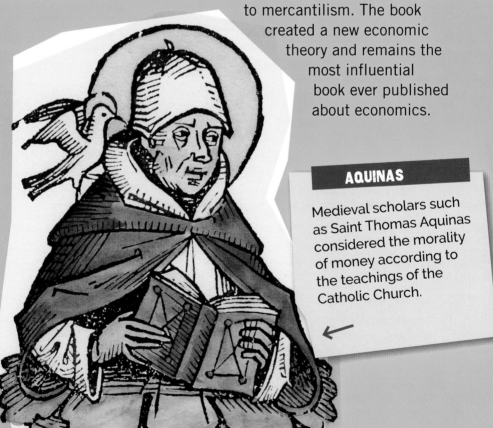

AQUINAS

Medieval scholars such as Saint Thomas Aquinas considered the morality of money according to the teachings of the Catholic Church.

←

ADAM SMITH

Adam Smith argued that nations should develop specialized industry depending on their resources, and then trade with their neighbors for other goods.

←

Smith argued that the global economy was not limited, as mercantilism suggested. It could keep growing endlessly to the benefit of all countries. There should be no restrictions on trade. Smith said an invisible hand, called the law of supply and demand, shaped the economy. If more people wanted a product, its price increased. If fewer people wanted it, the price fell. In that way, the economy regulated itself.

ECONOMIC THEORY TIMELINE

A series of economic theories has emerged since Adam Smith wrote the first economic study, *The Wealth of Nations*, in 1776.

1500s-1700s Mercantilism
1776 Free market
1798 Malthusianism
1848 Communism
1936 Keynesianism
1956 Monetarism

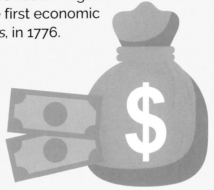

The impact of *The Wealth of Nations* was not felt immediately. However, by the 1800s Smith's theory of free trade had been adopted by most Western nations. Nations encouraged international trade rather than trying to limit it.

After Smith

In the 1800s, a number of other influential economists put forward economic ideas. David Ricardo expanded on Smith's argument that markets regulated themselves better than any government. The English cleric Thomas Malthus proposed that population growth did not lead to economic growth for all, leaving the poor to suffer. The German Karl Marx argued that there would always be conflict between workers and the employers who exploited them. He argued that workers needed to revolt and create a communist government that would control a country's economic activity for the good of everyone.

In the 1930s, the British economist John Maynard Keynes put forward his theories. He supported the free market, but said that an economy could not be totally unregulated.

MARXISM

Karl Marx's argument that workers should seize control of the economy laid the foundation for the rise of communism in the 1900s.

DEPRESSION

John Maynard Keynes argued in the 1930s that government action could prevent financial disasters like the Great **Depression**.

Keynes said that governments should use regulation to control an economy that was failing. In the 1950s, economists came up with a new theory called monetarism. This said that governments could influence free trade simply by making more or less money available in the economy. That remained a popular approach to economic policy at the end of the 20th century and into the 21st century.

IN SUMMARY

- The formal study of economic theory began in the late 1700s.

- Modern economic theories debate the level to which governments should be involved in economic activity, from complete control to control of the money supply to free trade.

THE GLOBAL AGE

Since the end of World War II in 1945, the world has changed beyond all recognition. Today, capitalism dominates the world's economies.

The end of World War I (1914–1918) had left Europe's economies in ruins. Political extremism emerged with communism in the Soviet Union and **fascism** in Italy and Germany. In the United States, the economy boomed in the 1920s until an attempt to protect U.S. industry by limiting imports from the rest of the world led to a slowing of global trade.

CRISIS

Dealers on the New York Stock Exchange watch as share prices fall during the financial crisis in 2008.

→

Trade slowed so much that it caused the Great Depression of 1929 to 1939. By 1933, U.S. unemployment had reached 25 percent. The effects of the depression spread around the world, demonstrating that the United States was part of a global economy. President Franklin D. Roosevelt's government employed thousands of people on public works projects. The government hoped these workers would use their earnings to buy goods, helping to stimulate trade.

The economy only returned to pre-depression levels when World War II (1939–1945) broke out. Millions of workers were needed to produce supplies for the war.

Prosperity for all?

At the end of World War II, the economies of much of Europe and Asia were again in ruins. This time, economists were careful to help the defeated countries of Germany and Japan recover quickly in order to stimulate demand for international trade.

TIMELINE

1929 The Great Depression begins when a decade of U.S. prosperity ends in a sudden economic decline.

1989 The countries of Eastern Europe abandon communism. The Soviet Union breaks up. Communist economies cannot compete with the free-market West.

2008 Banks lose billions of dollars through providing credit to those who cannot repay what they owe, leading to a global credit crisis.

37

In the 1930s and 1940s, the Soviet Union had created a communist economy. China did the same in the 1950s and 1960s. All economic activity was controlled by the government. The Soviet economy depended on heavy industry and agriculture. In China, millions of Chinese people were forced to live in collective villages and farm together. In 1989, the Soviet Union collapsed. The controlled economy had not worked. Soviet industry could not compete with U.S. industry, which became far more technologically advanced in the 1970s and 1980s.

Since the collapse of the Soviet Union, free-market economics have become the major international economic model. Few communist economies survive. In China, the Communist Party encourages Chinese citizens to act as **entrepreneurs** by setting up new businesses. The Chinese want to use their huge population to make China the manufacturing center for the world.

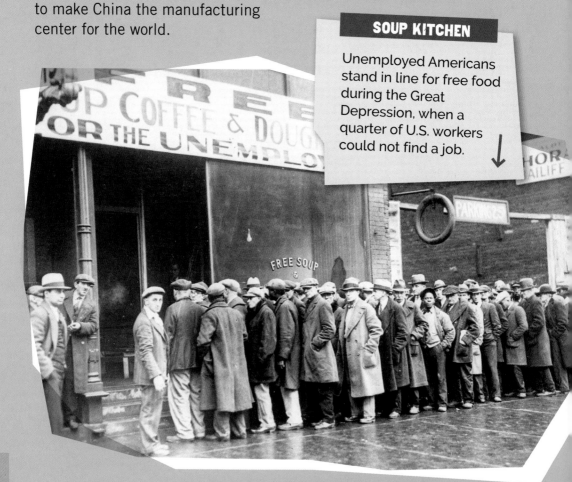

SOUP KITCHEN

Unemployed Americans stand in line for free food during the Great Depression, when a quarter of U.S. workers could not find a job. ↓

BOOMING

Workers open new oil pipelines during a period of economic expansion in the United States during the 1950s. The postwar boom created great optimism for many. →

Trading blocs

Since World War II, countries have formed free-trade blocs, or groups of countries that do not tax each other's goods. They include the European Union (EU) and the North American Free Trade Agreement (NAFTA). However, some countries still impose **tariffs** on imported goods. They hope these duties will protect their own industries. Free trade has stimulated economic growth, but it has also led to hardship. For example, the steel industries in Britain and the United States have suffered because steel is cheaper to manufacture in India and China. British and U.S. steelworkers have lost their jobs as a result.

WEALTH DISTRIBUTION

The distribution of wealth remains uneven. The richest 1 percent of the global population own half of the world's wealth.

Average annual income of the world's wealthiest people

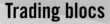

TOP 1% $759,900

TOP 10% $68,800

TOP 50% $3,210

Money in the global age

Since the 1980s, a technological revolution has transformed the way business is done and the way money changes hands. It is possible to pay for things without handling any actual money. The Internet makes it easier to move money around than ever before.

One consequence of the increased circulation of money was a rise in credit. Credit is when people borrow money on the condition that they will repay the money in the future with interest. In the 2000s, complex financial arrangements encouraged U.S. banks to give credit to many people who were not in a position to repay their debts. In 2008, this led to a credit crisis. U.S. and foreign banks came close to collapse. The financial crisis that followed is still being felt. Governments spent billions of dollars to stop banks and other institutions from going bust. This was an unusually direct way for governments to become involved in the economy in the modern world.

OCCUPY

Protestors against the global economy and the international banking system in New York City during the Occupy movement of 2011.

↓

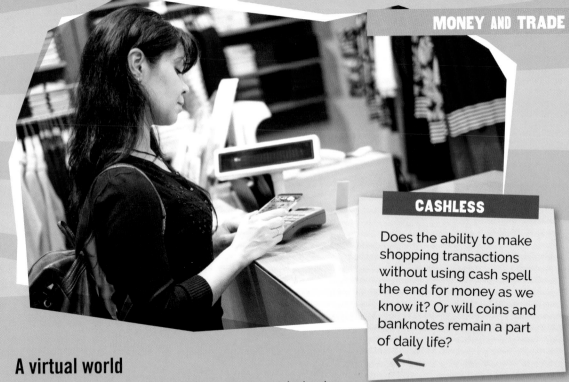

CASHLESS

Does the ability to make shopping transactions without using cash spell the end for money as we know it? Or will coins and banknotes remain a part of daily life?

←

A virtual world

Ancient peoples believed that money only had worth if it was made from precious metals. The idea that we buy and sell goods via computers and smartphones without ever seeing the cash would be unbelievable to them. The modern economy is cashless. People no longer need to take real money when they leave home. At the same time, money is more important than ever. The gulf between those who have money and those who do not is wider than ever— and seems set to continue growing wider.

IN SUMMARY

■ After World War I, international trade revived only slowly, helping to trigger the Great Depression.

■ Although communism was discredited as an economic theory, free-market economics remained vulnerable to crises, as in the global credit crisis that began in 2008.

THE WORLD TODAY

Today many countries are members of regional trade blocs. These allow trade between members without the charge of tariffs.

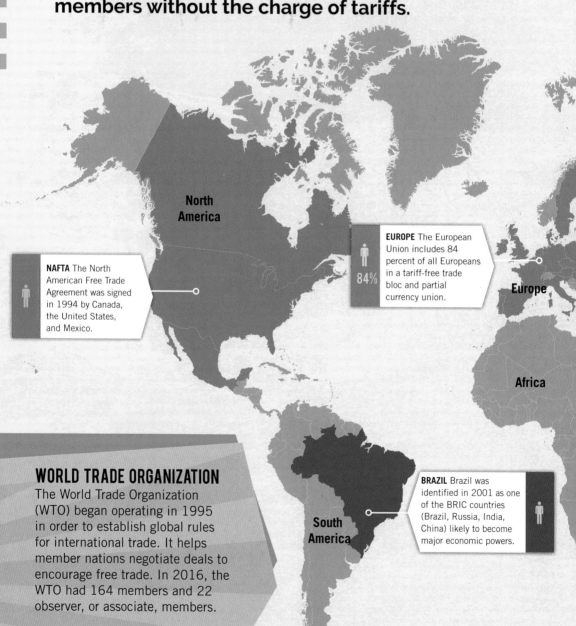

North America

NAFTA The North American Free Trade Agreement was signed in 1994 by Canada, the United States, and Mexico.

EUROPE The European Union includes 84 percent of all Europeans in a tariff-free trade bloc and partial currency union.

84%

Europe

Africa

WORLD TRADE ORGANIZATION

The World Trade Organization (WTO) began operating in 1995 in order to establish global rules for international trade. It helps member nations negotiate deals to encourage free trade. In 2016, the WTO had 164 members and 22 observer, or associate, members.

South America

BRAZIL Brazil was identified in 2001 as one of the BRIC countries (Brazil, Russia, India, China) likely to become major economic powers.

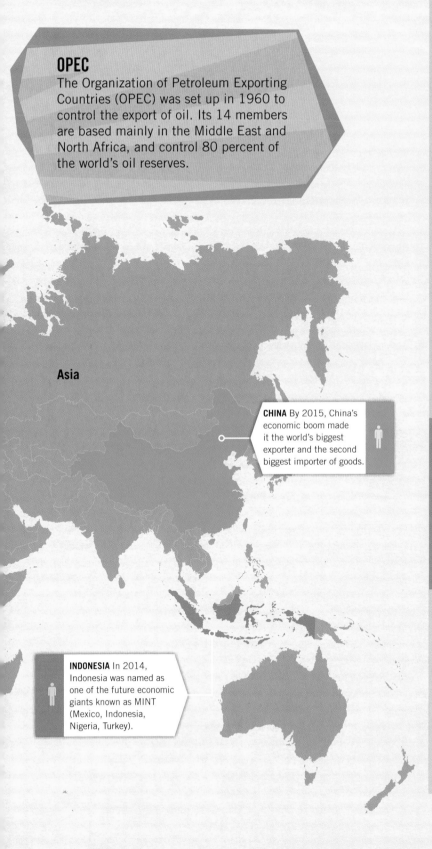

OPEC

The Organization of Petroleum Exporting Countries (OPEC) was set up in 1960 to control the export of oil. Its 14 members are based mainly in the Middle East and North Africa, and control 80 percent of the world's oil reserves.

Asia

CHINA By 2015, China's economic boom made it the world's biggest exporter and the second biggest importer of goods.

INDONESIA In 2014, Indonesia was named as one of the future economic giants known as MINT (Mexico, Indonesia, Nigeria, Turkey).

TIMELINE

ca. 12,000 BCE — Obsidian is traded widely around the Mediterranean from its sources in Anatolia and on various islands.

ca. 3000 BCE — Trade is well established on many of the rivers of the ancient world, including the Nile in Egypt, the Indus in India, and the Yellow River in China.

ca. 3000 BCE — The Sumerians begin to use silver ingots for trade. Silver is weighed in official units called shekels.

ca. 1000 BCE — Traders establish overland routes across Asia, including the Silk Road, which connects China and South Asia to the Mediterranean Sea.

ca. 640 BCE — The Lydians of what is now Turkey make the world's first coins. The coins carry a stamped lion, the symbol of the Lydian king, as a sign that they are genuine.

476 CE — The collapse of the Roman Empire in the West leads to a dramatic reduction of trade in Europe.

600s — The Chinese begin printing the first paper money. It is initially created by merchants as receipts, but is later printed by the government.

700s — Viking traders open trade routes around the coasts of northern Europe and via rivers into what is now Russia.

1000s — The Republic of Venice controls the Adriatic Sea, allowing it to build an empire based on trade with Islamic states in the eastern Mediterranean.

1492 — Trying to find a new sea route to Asia, Christopher Columbus sails to the Caribbean, opening trade routes between Europe and the Americas.

1600 — British traders form the East India Company to develop trade with India and East Asia.

1500s	Envious of Spain and its gold and silver reserves from South America, European nations adopt mercantilist policies.
ca. 1550	The African slave trade with the Americas begins to grow in scale. Around 10 million Africans are seized and enslaved.
1776	Adam Smith publishes *The Wealth of Nations*, setting out the theory of free-market economics. The book begins the study of economics in its own right.
1842	British victory in the First Opium War forces the Chinese to allow foreigners to trade in China. In the next decade, Japan also permits international trade.
1848	Germans Karl Marx and Friedrich Engels publish *The Communist Manifesto*. It is widely banned and makes little initial impact.
1860s	The building of railroads in the West in the United States leads to the creation of a huge business based on cattle herds and meat production in Chicago.
1901	Andrew Carnegie sells the Carnegie Steel Company to J. P. Morgan for $492 million, making him temporarily the richest man in America.
1929	The Great Depression begins when a decade of U.S. prosperity ends in a sudden economic decline.
1989	The countries of Eastern Europe abandon communism, followed by the breakup of the Soviet Union. Communist economies cannot compete with the free-market West.
2008	Banks lose billions of dollars through providing credit to those who cannot repay what they owe, leading to a global credit crisis.
2016	Britain votes to leave the European Union. Donald Trump is elected U.S. president after promising to change U.S. trade deals with countries such as China and Mexico.

GLOSSARY

barter To exchange goods or services for other goods or services.

Bitcoin A type of digital currency.

colonies Regions or countries wholly governed by a foreign country.

commercial Something done in order to make money.

commodities Raw materials and agricultural products that are traded.

communism A system of social organization in which all property is owned by the community.

consumers People who buy goods and services for their own use.

corporations Large companies or groups of companies that act as a single body.

credit The ability to gain goods or services on the understanding that the seller will pay in the future.

currency A system of money in use in a particular country.

depression A long and severe slowdown in economic activity.

economics The branch of knowledge concerned with the production, use, and transfer of wealth.

entrepreneurs People who take risks by setting up businesses in the hopes of earning a profit.

exports Products and services sold abroad.

fascism An authoritarian and nationalistic form of government.

free market Describes an economy in which there are no regulations on trade.

functional Related to the purpose or use of something.

ingots Blocks of gold, silver, or other metals.

interest A sum of money paid in return for borrowing money.

investors People who fund a venture in the hopes of making money in the future.

lagoon An area of salt water separated from the sea by a sandbank.

maritime Related to the sea.

mercantilism An economic theory based on the accumulation of wealth.

metallurgy The science of metals and their properties.

moral Related to ideas of good and bad behavior.

multinational Operating in more than one country.

nomadic Having no fixed residence.

philosopher Someone who thinks about profound issues of life and existence.

plantations Large farms used to grow crops.

railheads Places where railroads meet roads or other transportation routes.

receipts Written documents confirming the exchange of goods or money.

supply and demand The amount of something that is available and the desire of buyers for it, which together determine its selling price.

surplus More than is needed of something.

tariffs Payments that have to be made on imported or exported goods.

FURTHER RESOURCES

Books

Crain, Cynthia D. and Dwight R. Lee. *Adam Smith*. Profiles in Economics. Greensboro: Morgan Reynolds Publishing, 2009.

Dolezalek. Holly. *The Global Financial Crisis*. Essential Events. Edina: Abdo Publishing Company, 2011.

Pascal, Janet. *What Was the Great Depression?* New York: Franklin Watts, 2015.

Rice, Dona Herweck. *Buy It! History of: Money*. Huntington Beach: Teacher Created Materials, 2014.

Richardson, Hazel. *Trade and Commerce in the Ancient World*. Life in the Ancient World. New York: Crabtree Publishing, 2015.

Woolf, Alex. *You Wouldn't Want to Live Without Money!* New York: Franklin Watts, 2015.

Websites

www.ducksters.com/history/china/silk_road.php
This Ducksters page provides information about the Silk Road, the great trade route that connected China and the Mediterranean.

www.ducksters.com/money/adam_smith.php
This biography of the economist Adam Smith summarizes some of his most influential ideas.

keynesforkids.com/
This interactive site about the economic theories of John Maynard Keynes features quizzes and activities.

www.kidspast.com/world-history/0066B-development-of-money-2.php
The information on this page explains how bartering works and how money developed over time.

http://www.socialstudiesforkids.com/subjects/economics.htm
This website provides links to additional information about economics.

http://wiki.kidzsearch.com/wiki/Economics
This article about economics for kids provides links to pages about the history of economics.

INDEX